A Children's Book About
LYING

Grolier Enterprises, Inc. offers a varied selection of children's
book racks and tote bags. For details on ordering, please write:
Grolier Enterprises Inc., Sherman Turnpike, Danbury, CT 06816
Attn: Premium Department

Managing Editor: Ellen Klarberg
Copy Editor: Annette Gooch
Editorial Assistant: Lana Eberhard
Art Director: Jennifer Wiezel
Production Artist: Gail Miller
Illustration Designer: Bartholomew
Inking Artist: Micah Schwaberow
Coloring Artist: Susie Hornig
Lettering Artist: Linda Hanney
Typographer: Communication Graphics

Printed in 1991

A Children's Book About

LYING

By Joy Berry

GROLIER ENTERPRISES CORP.

This book is about Katie.

Reading about Katie can help you understand and deal with **lying**.

Sometimes you might make up a story and tell it to other people for fun.

An untrue story that is told for fun is called a *fantasy*.

It is OK to tell a fantasy. But it is important to remember that the fantasy is not true. It is also important to make sure that others know it is not true.

Sometimes you might say something you think is true. Then later you might discover that what you said is not true.

When you do not know that what you are saying is untrue, you are making a mistake.

It is OK to make mistakes because no one is perfect. Everyone makes mistakes.

Sometimes you might purposely tell someone something that is not true. When you do this:

- You are not telling a fantasy.
- You are not making a mistake.
- You are lying.

Lying is trying to make someone believe something that is not true. It is *deceiving* or *fooling* someone on purpose.

Lying is not a good thing to do. When you lie:

- You disappoint other people.
- You cause people to wonder if you ever tell the truth.
- You cause people to stop trusting you.

People who do not trust you might not believe you when you are telling the truth.

This is not good. There are times when you need to have people believe you.

So, you should not lie.

There are many ways to tell lies. You can tell lies *with your actions.*

You might cause someone to believe something that is not true by acting a certain way. You are lying when you do this.

You can tell lies *with your silence.*

You might cause someone to believe something that is not true by not saying anything. You are lying when you do this.

You can tell lies *with your words.*

You might cause someone to believe
something by saying things that are untrue.
You are lying when you do this.

People usually find out when you lie to them.

Do not try to cover up a lie by telling more lies. This will only make things worse.

Tell the truth if you have lied.

Admit that you have lied. Say "I lied to you."
This will begin to make things better.

Say that you are sorry if you have lied.

Do everything you can do to show you are truly sorry you lied.

Then do not tell any more lies.

If you want people to believe and trust you, you must not lie to them.